WORSHIP GRAFFITI

FAITH BUILDING

ACTIVITY JOURNAL

Greg Bretz

Halo
PUBLISHING
INTERNATIONAL

ISBN: 978-1-61244-886-2

Halo Publishing International, LLC
8000 W Interstate 10, Suite 600
San Antonio, Texas 78230
www.halopublishing.com

Printed and bound in the United States

Introduction

Worship Graffiti – Faith Building Activity Journal has activities equipped to give you a creative outlet to study God's Word and learn about His love for you. If you are struggling, discouraged, or simply need a fun and inspiring activity, I know you will enjoy this new and exciting outlet. You will dive into the message of God's love for us. I wrote this from my own experience needing a visual representation for inspiration.

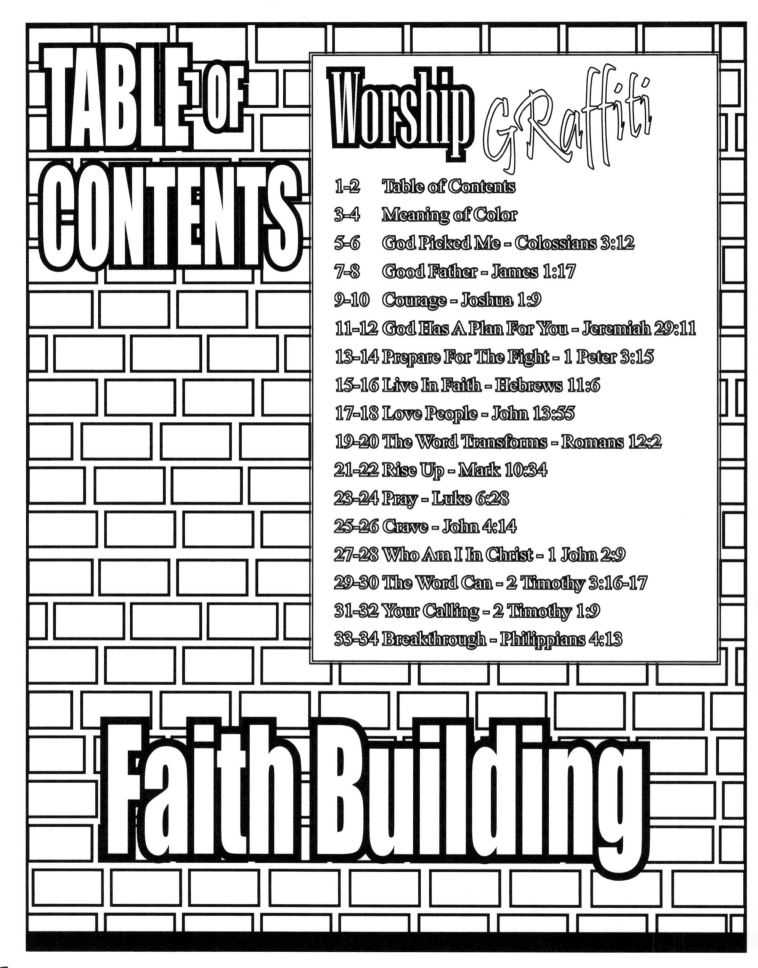

TABLE OF CONTENTS

Worship GRaffiti

Faith Building

TABLE OF CONTENTS

Worship GRaffiti

Activity Journal

WHAT IS Color?

A SPECIFIC COMBINATION OF HUE, SATURATION, AND LIGHTNESS OR BRIGHTNESS

RED - excitement, energy, love, speed, strength, POWER, intensity, and passion

Orange - energy, enthusiasm, warmth, and vibrance

DON'T SIT ON YOUR GIFT!

GOLD - love, compassion, courage, and passion

Yellow - joy, happiness, hope, and friendship

Green - health, renewal, youth, and generosity

Blue - peace, calm, stability, trust, truth, security, order, and loyalty

Purple - royalty, nobility, spirituality, transformation, wisdom, and honor

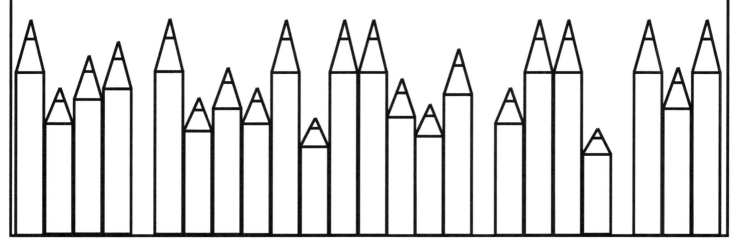

5

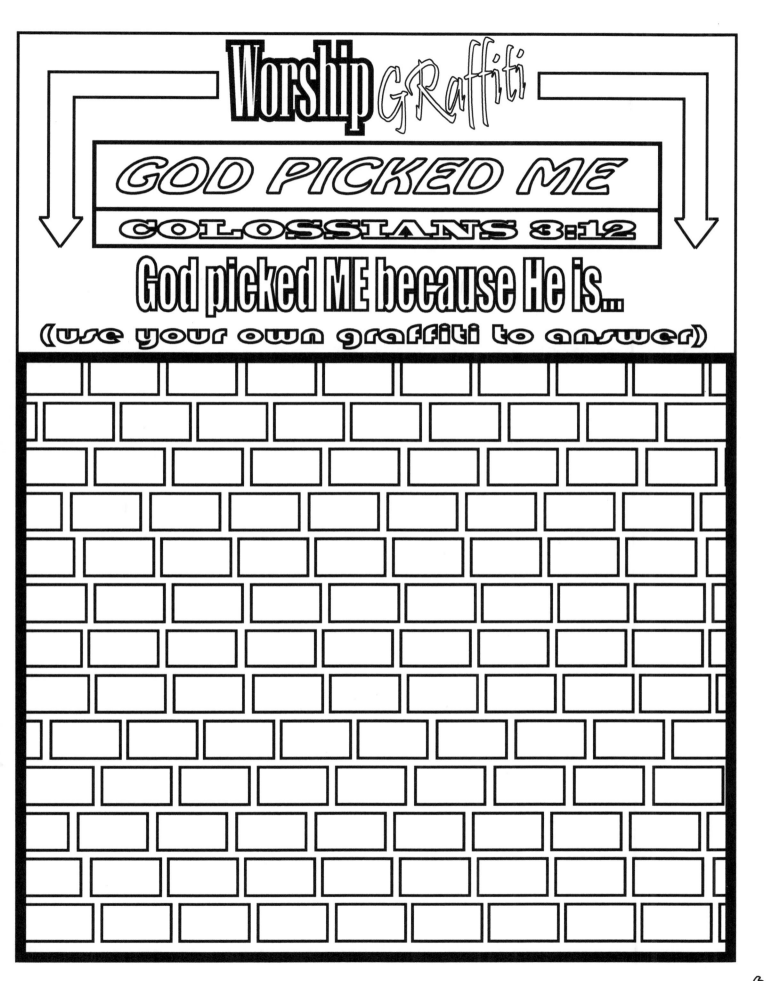

Worship GRaffiti

GOD PICKED ME
COLOSSIANS 3:12

God picked ME because He is...
(use your own graffiti to answer)

6

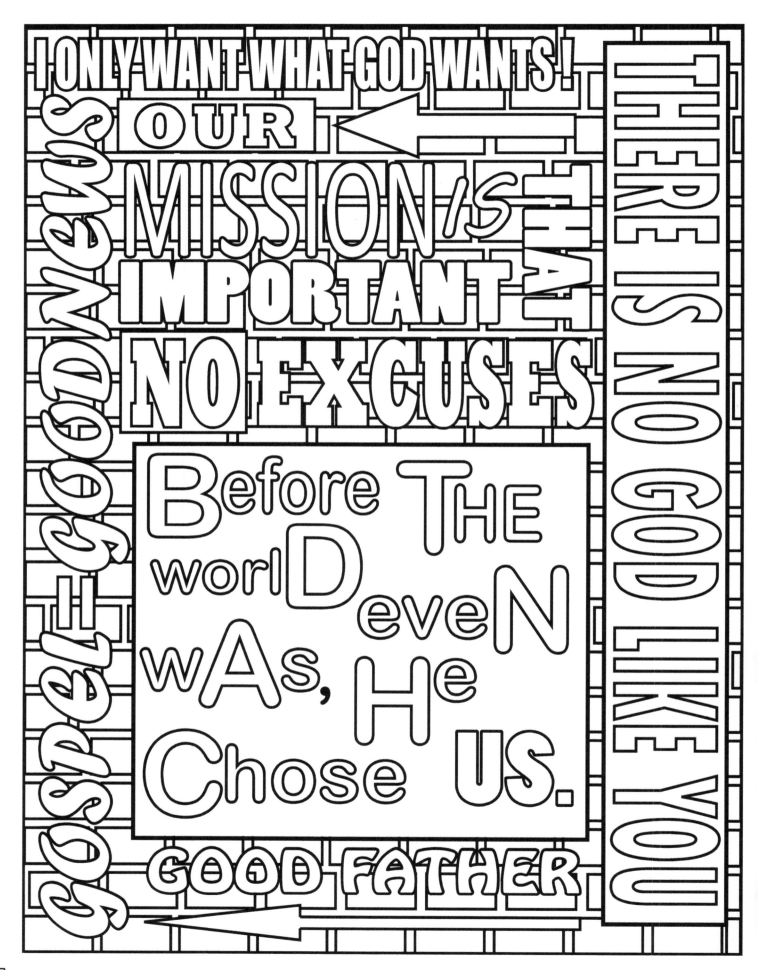

7

NO FEAR!

DO YOU ACCEPT THE CALL?

OVERCOME EVIL WITH GOOD

RESCUED FROM DARKNESS

TRANSFORMED

"for God gave us a spirit not of fear but of power and love and self-control"

COURAGE!!!

not-not-not-not ASHAMED

2 TIMOTHY 1:7 ESV

Worship GRaffiti

COURAGE

Joshua 1:9

Areas where I need COURAGE...

(use your own graffiti to answer)

Worship GRaffiti

GOD HAS A PLAN FOR YOU

Jeremiah 29:11

Gods plans for ME look like...
(use your own graffiti to answer)

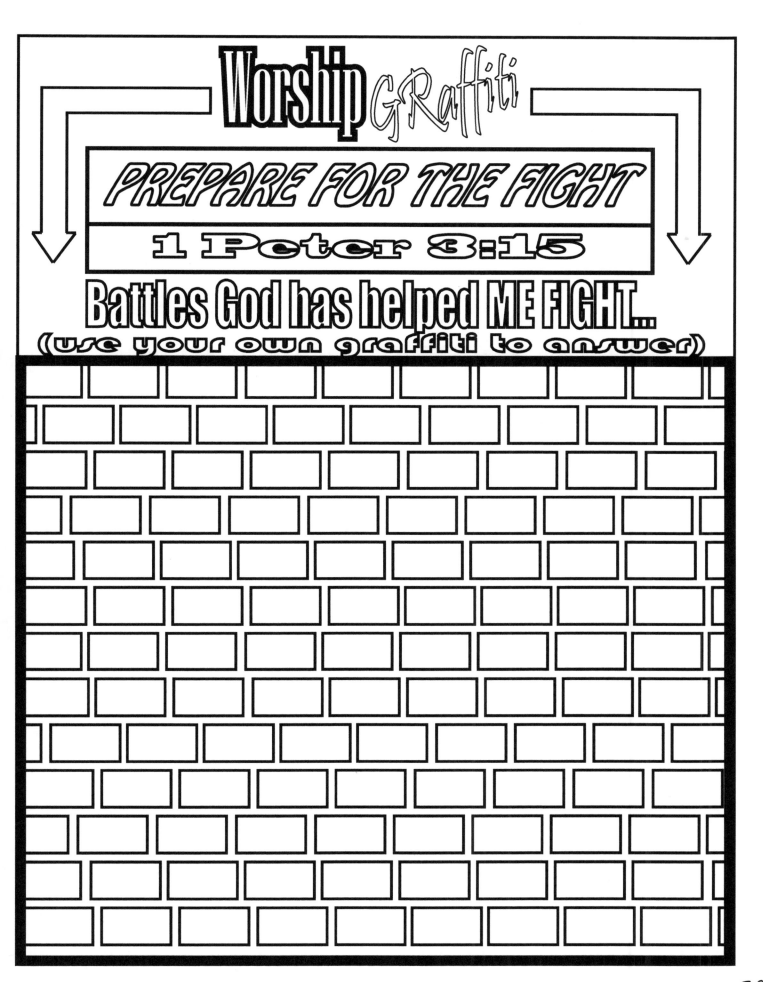

Worship GRaffiti

PREPARE FOR THE FIGHT

1 Peter 3:15

Battles God has helped ME FIGHT...

(use your own graffiti to answer)

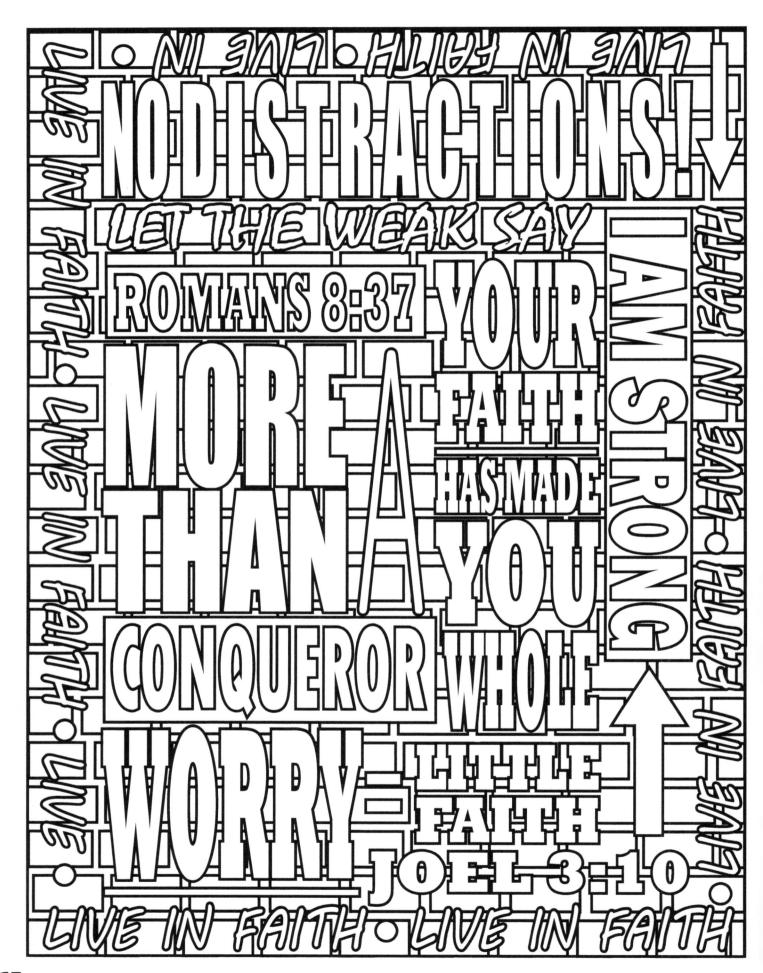

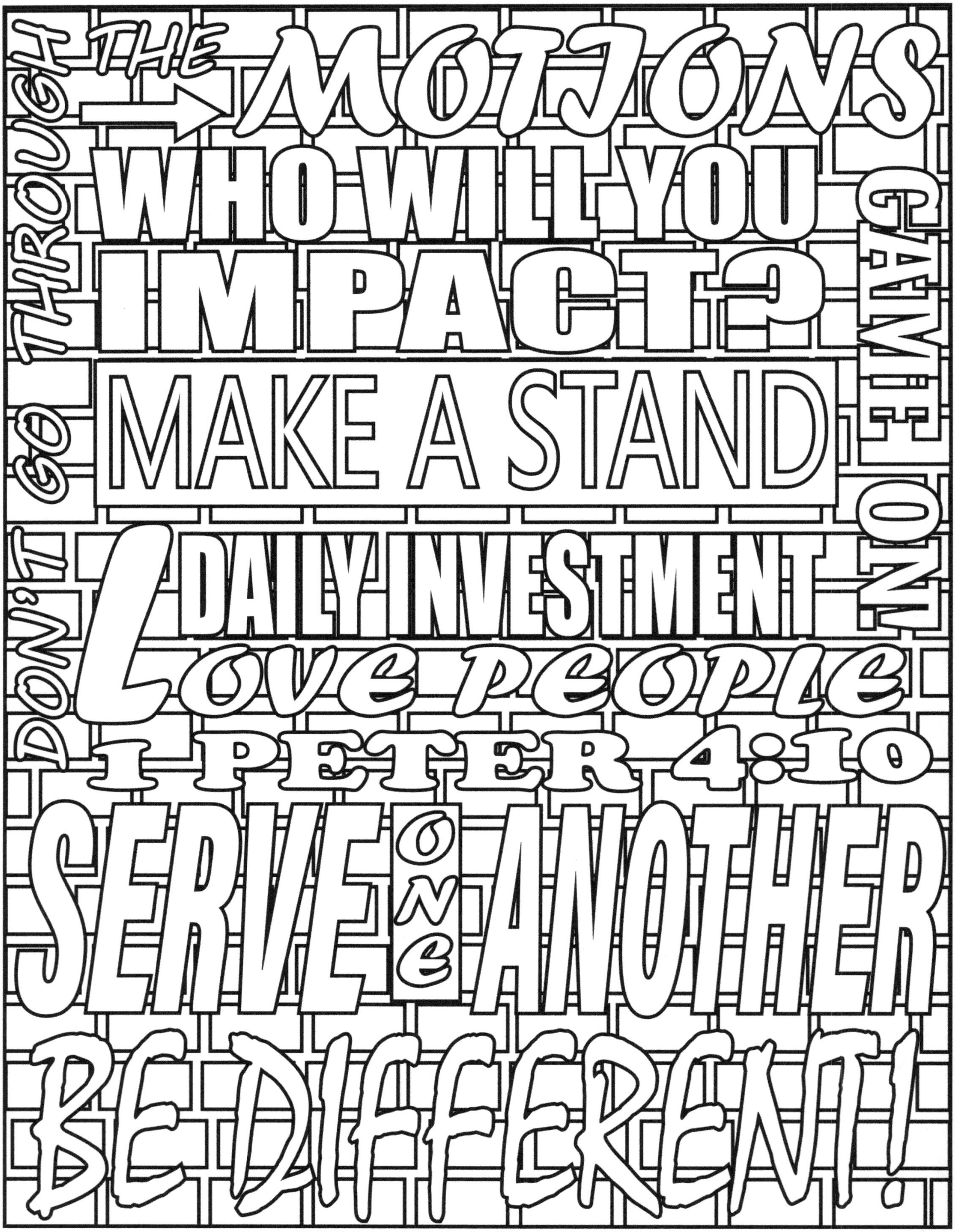
DON'T GO THROUGH THE MOTIONS
WHO WILL YOU IMPACT?
MAKE A STAND
GAME ON!
DAILY INVESTMENT
LOVE PEOPLE
1 PETER 4:10
SERVE ONE ANOTHER
BE DIFFERENT!

Worship GRaffiti

LOVE PEOPLE
John 13:55

How I can LOVE people...
(use your own graffiti to answer)

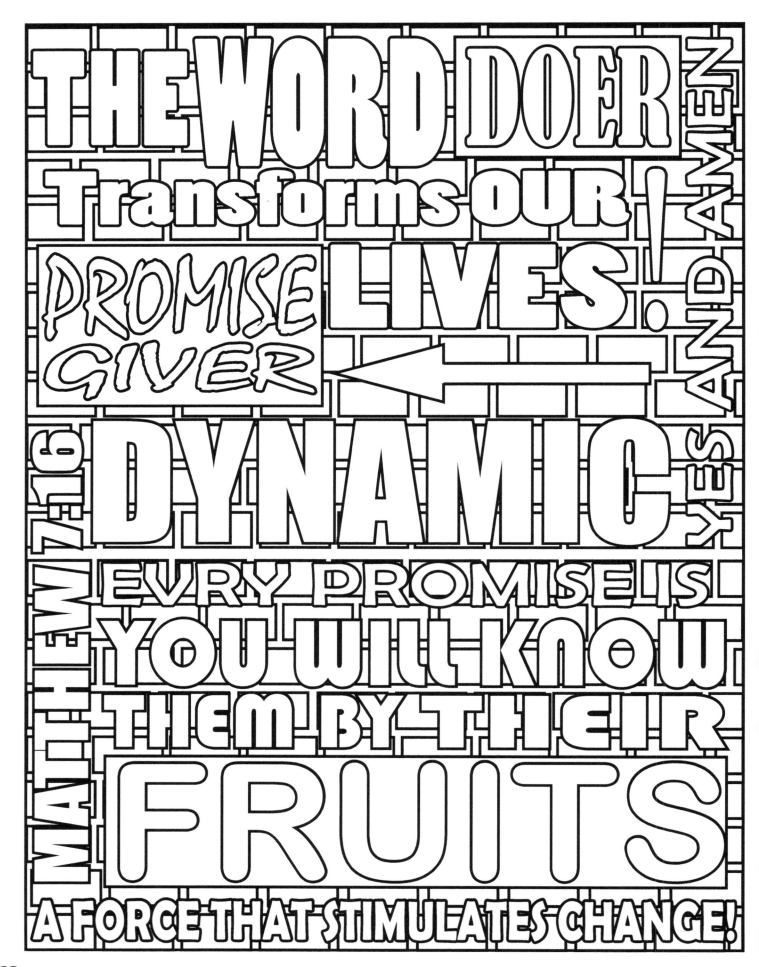

THE WORD DOER

Transforms OUR LIVES!

PROMISE GIVER

DYNAMIC

MATTHEW 7:16

YES AND AMEN

EVRY PROMISE IS YOU WILL KNOW THEM BY THEIR FRUITS

A FORCE THAT STIMULATES CHANGE!

19

Worship GRaffiti

THE WORD TRANSFORMS
Romans 12:2

Ways God has worked in my life...
(use your own graffiti to answer)

20

RISE UP!
EXODUS 40:33
FINISH THE
WORK
PREPARE FOR
BATTLE
BE → DIFFERENT
CONFIDENT
RIGHT HERE RIGHT NOW
You Are CALLED
STAND
MARK 8:34
TAKE UP HIS
CROSS AND
FOLLOW ME.
GET UP AND GO!

21

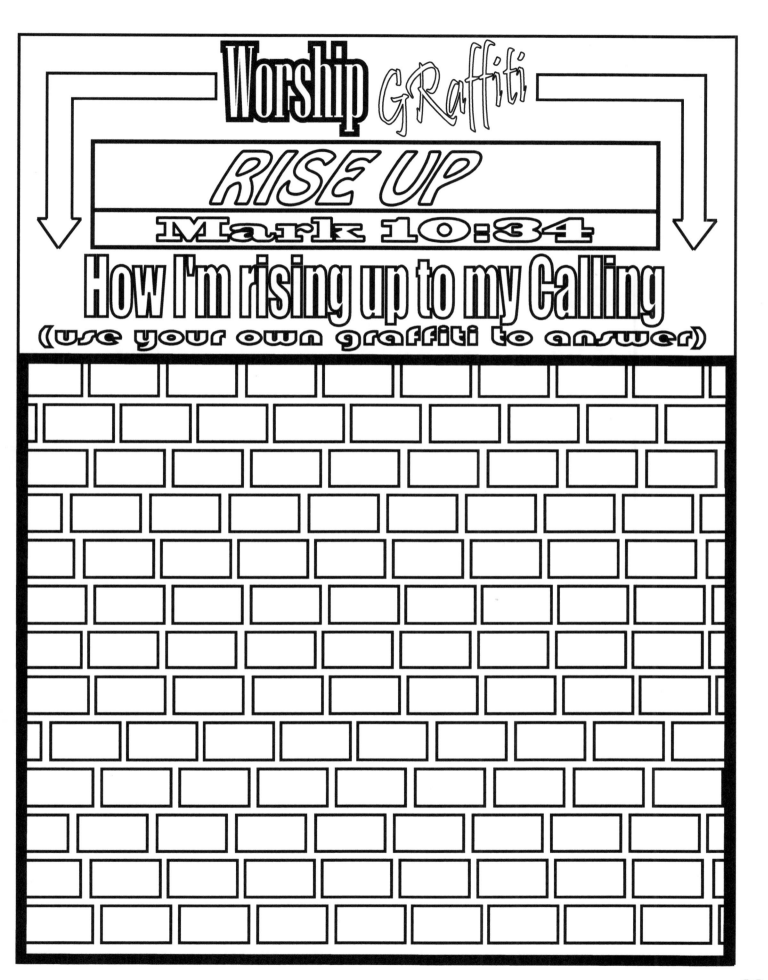

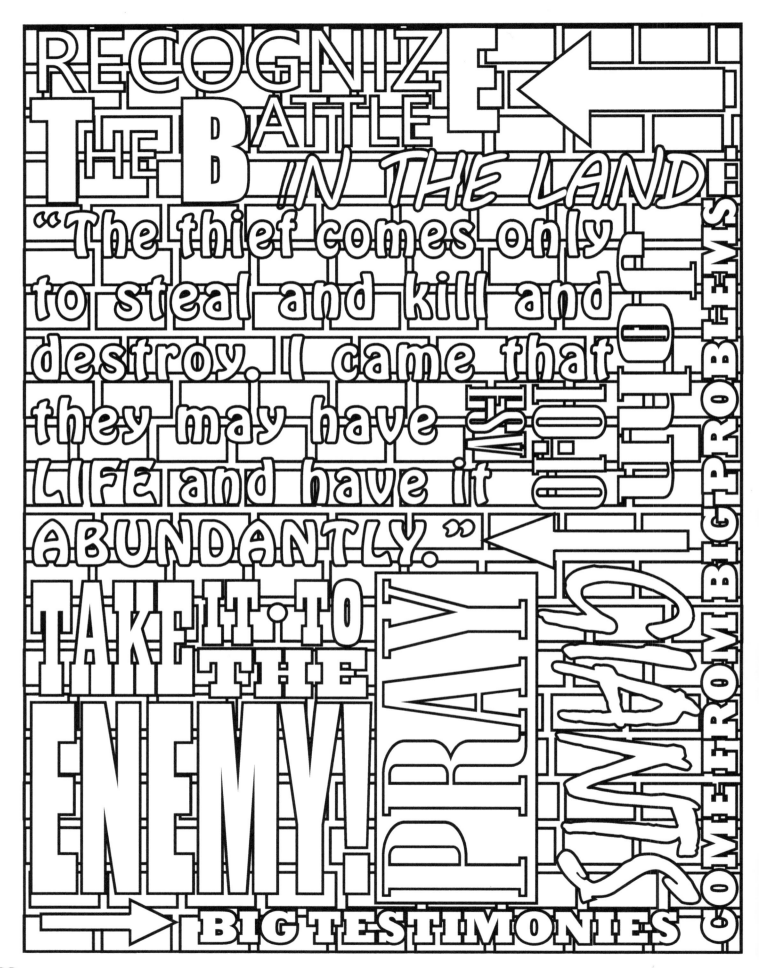

RECOGNIZE THE BATTLE IN THE LAND

"The thief comes only to steal and kill and destroy. I came that they may have LIFE and have it ABUNDANTLY."

JOHN 10:10

SOLUTION COME FROM BIG PROBLEMS

GIANTS

TAKE IT·TO THE ENEMY!

PRAY THIS

BIG TESTIMONIES

BE OF GOOD COURAGE

DON'T FEED THE WEED !

· PSALM 27:14

"LET NOT YOUR HEART TROUBLED." JOHN 14:1-3 ESV

BE BRAVE

CRAVE AN UPPER ROOM EXPERIENCE

DEAD TO SIN

GO DEEP WITH GOD

EXPECT

DRIVE YOUR DOWN ROOTS IN HIM

25

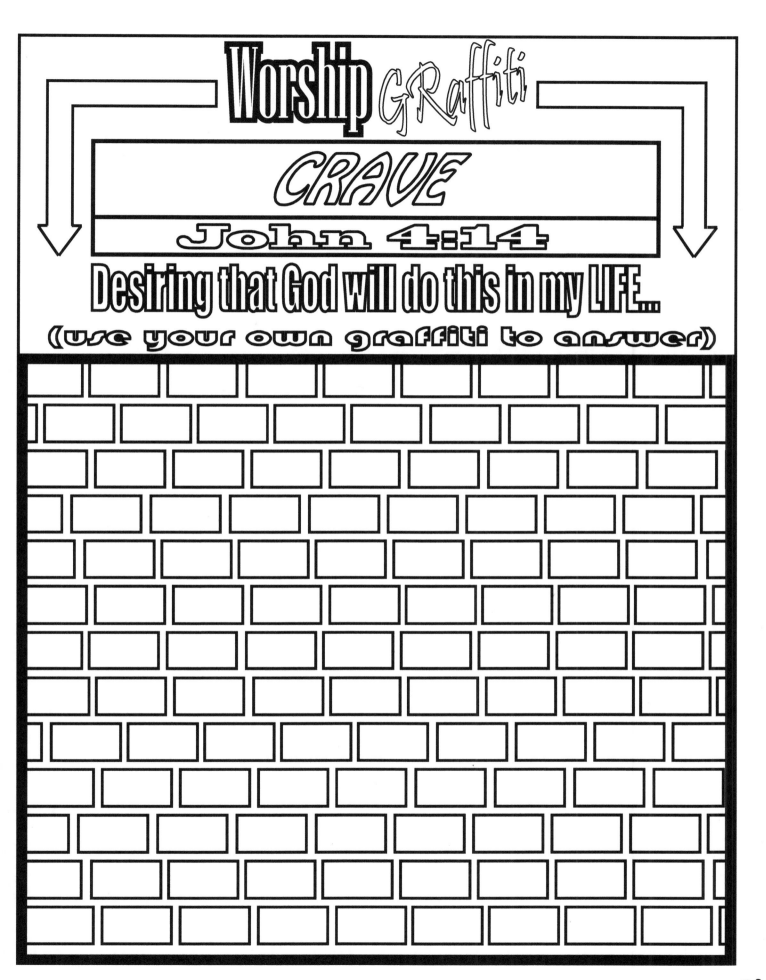

Worship GRaffiti

CRAVE

John 4:14

Desiring that God will do this in my LIFE...

(use your own graffiti to answer)

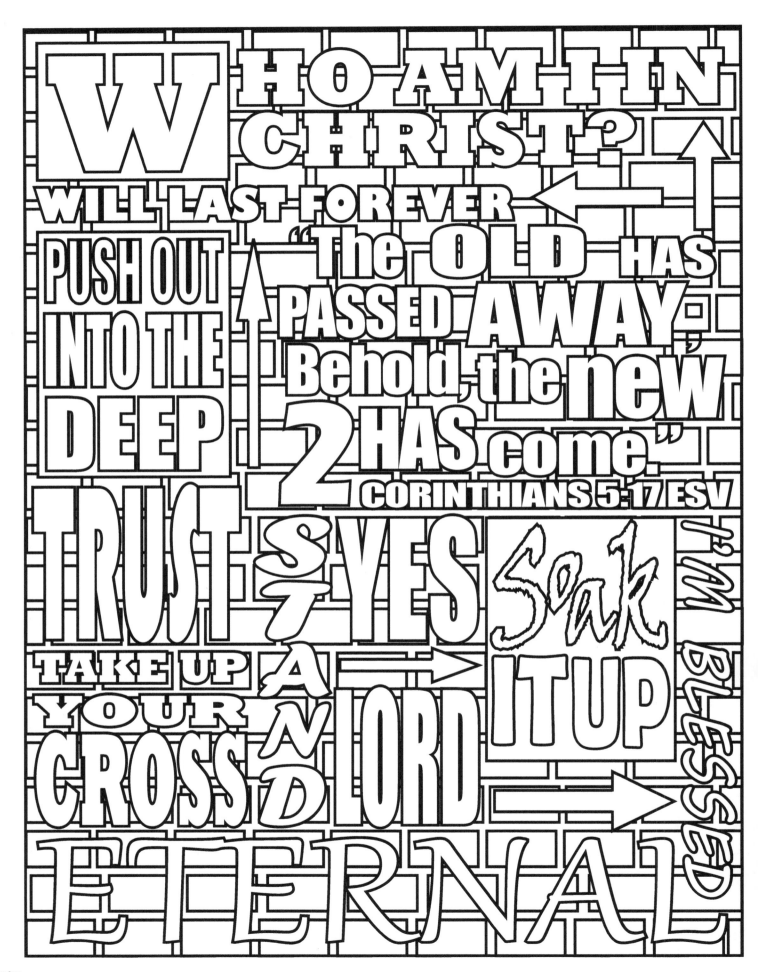

WHO AM I IN CHRIST?

WILL LAST FOREVER

PUSH OUT INTO THE DEEP

"The OLD HAS PASSED AWAY. Behold, the new 2 HAS come."

CORINTHIANS 5:17 ESV

TRUST

STAND YES

Soak IT UP

I'M BLESSED

TAKE UP YOUR CROSS AND LORD

ETERNAL

Worship GRaffiti

WHO AM I IN CHRIST

1 John 2:9

Who I am in God's family...

(use your own graffiti to answer)

THE *victory* WORD CAN BECOME *FLESH* JOHN 1-14

SCRIPTURE SAYS I CAN

SET THE COURSE ENGAGE

DAILY INVESTMENT GOD'S WORD IS ALIVE! GUIDE

STIMULATES CHANGE

29

Worship GRaffiti

THE WORD CAN

2 Timothy 3:16-17

The Word of God speaks this to me...

(use your own graffiti to answer)

DON'T SIT ON YOUR GIFT

TEST

PREPARE FOR IT

HAVE YOU

CALLING THE

CREATIVITY

FIND YOUR

DELIGHT

GOD IS COMMITTED ARE YOU?

BIRTH DREAMS

STEP OUT

DON'T WORRY ABOUT WHAT OTHERS SAY...

31

33

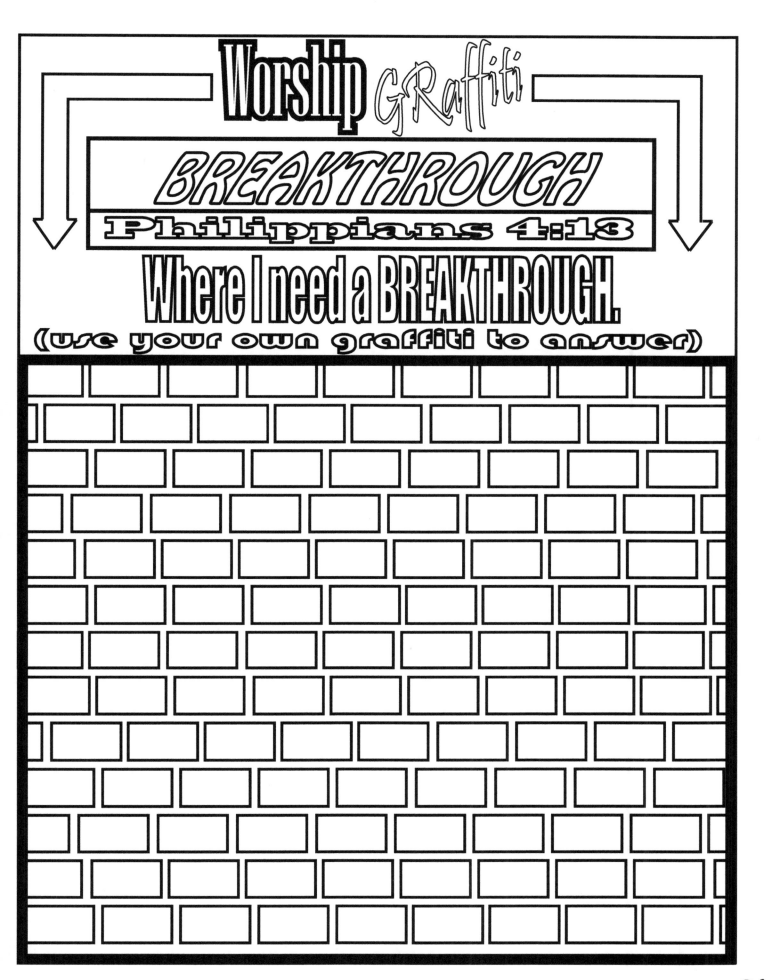

Worship GRaffiti

BREAKTHROUGH
Philippians 4:13

Where I need a BREAKTHROUGH.

(use your own graffiti to answer)

Worship GRaffiti

SPEAK LIFE
John 6:47

Ways I can encourage...
(use your own graffiti to answer)

36

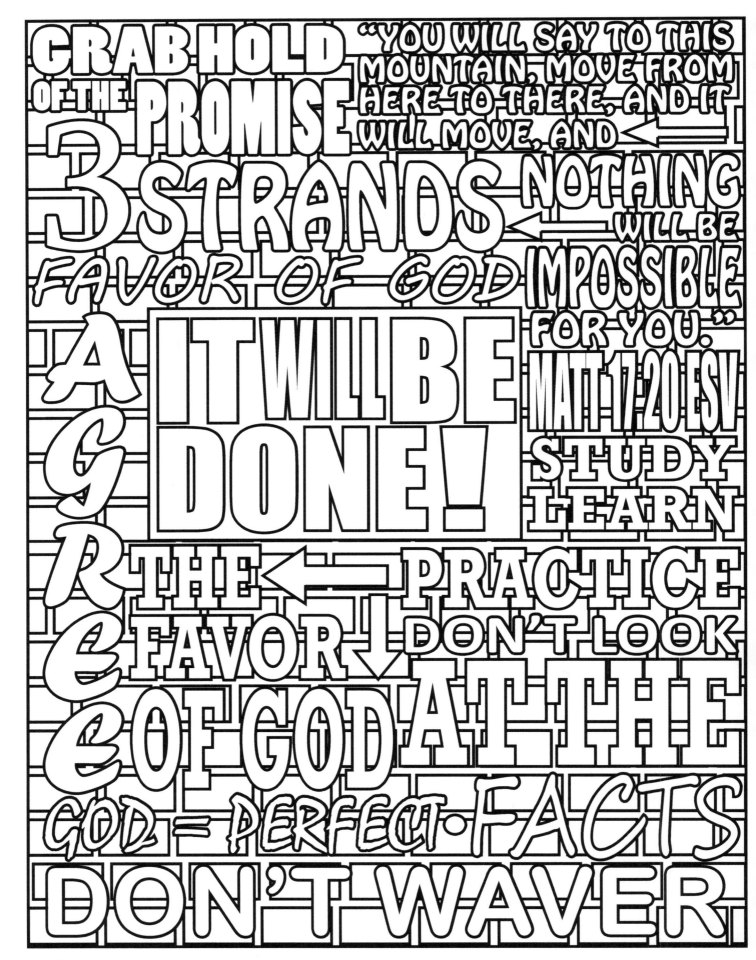

Worship GRaffiti

FAVOR OF GOD

Ephesians 1:11

Ways God has shown me favor

(use your own graffiti to answer)

38

39

Worship GRaffiti

HE IS GOOD

Psalm 136:1

Ways God has been good to me

(use your own graffiti to answer)

40

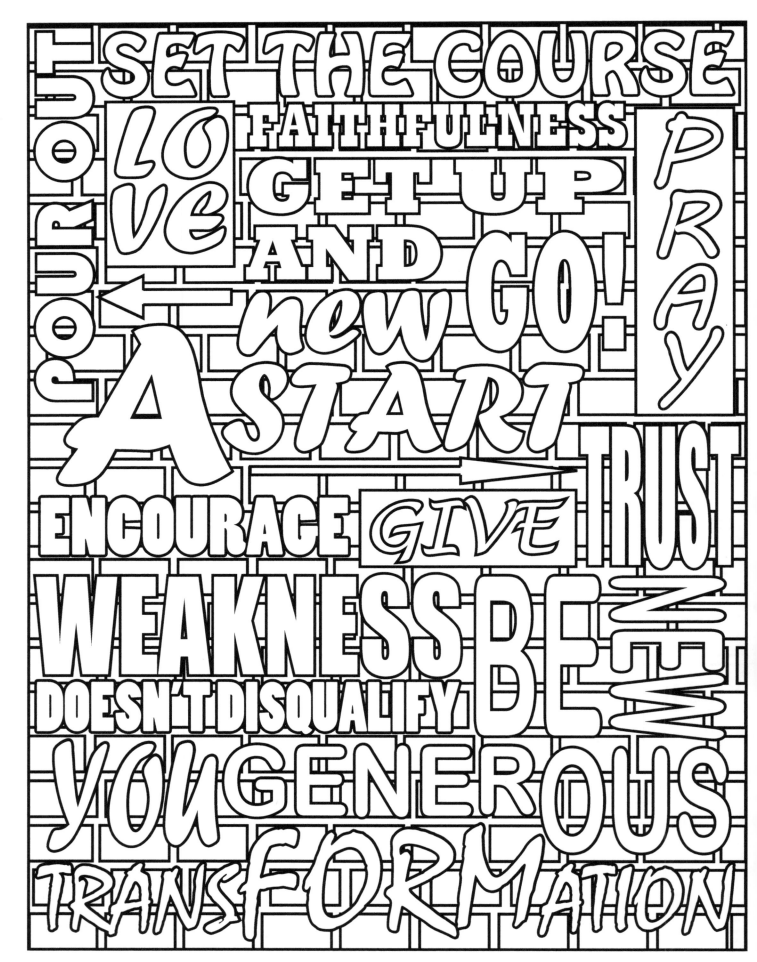

41

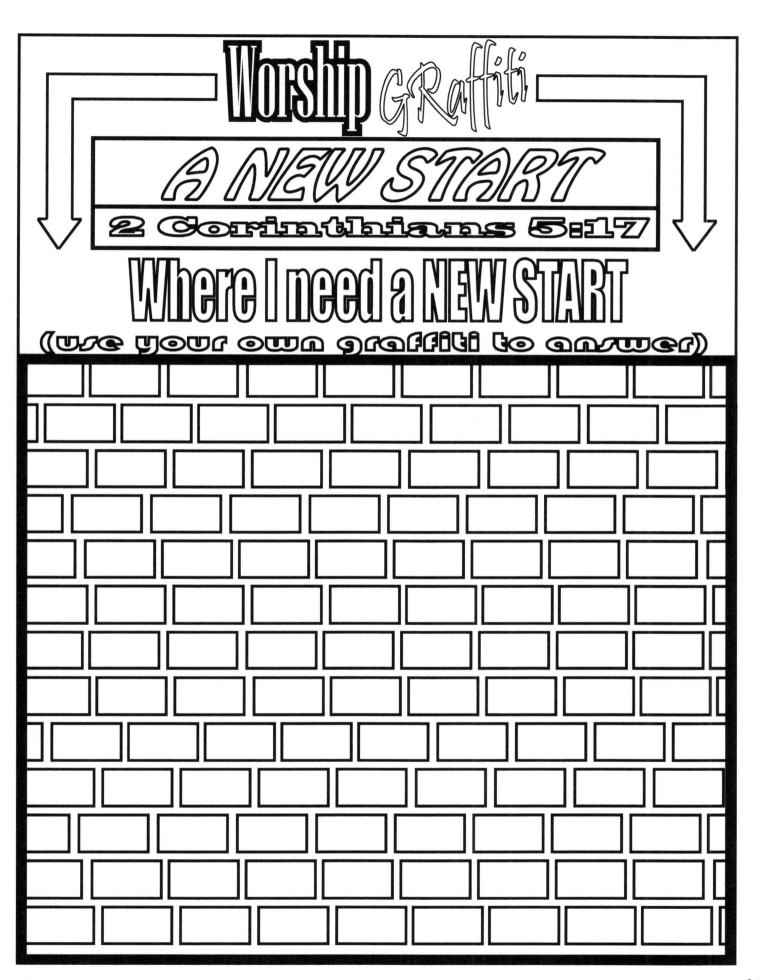

Worship GRaffiti

A NEW START
2 Corinthians 5:17

Where I need a NEW START
(use your own graffiti to answer)

SATIFIES

OTHERS

LOVE OTHERS

ME YOU·EVERYONE

IT'S GIVES

GOD'S PEACE

JOHN 3:16 ESV

ALL

AVAILABLE

"for GOD SO LOVED the World, that HE GAVE HIS only son."

FREE GIFT

EXCEEDS ALL

Worship GRaffiti

GOD'S LOVE
John 3:16
Ways God shows us His love...
(use your own graffiti to answer)

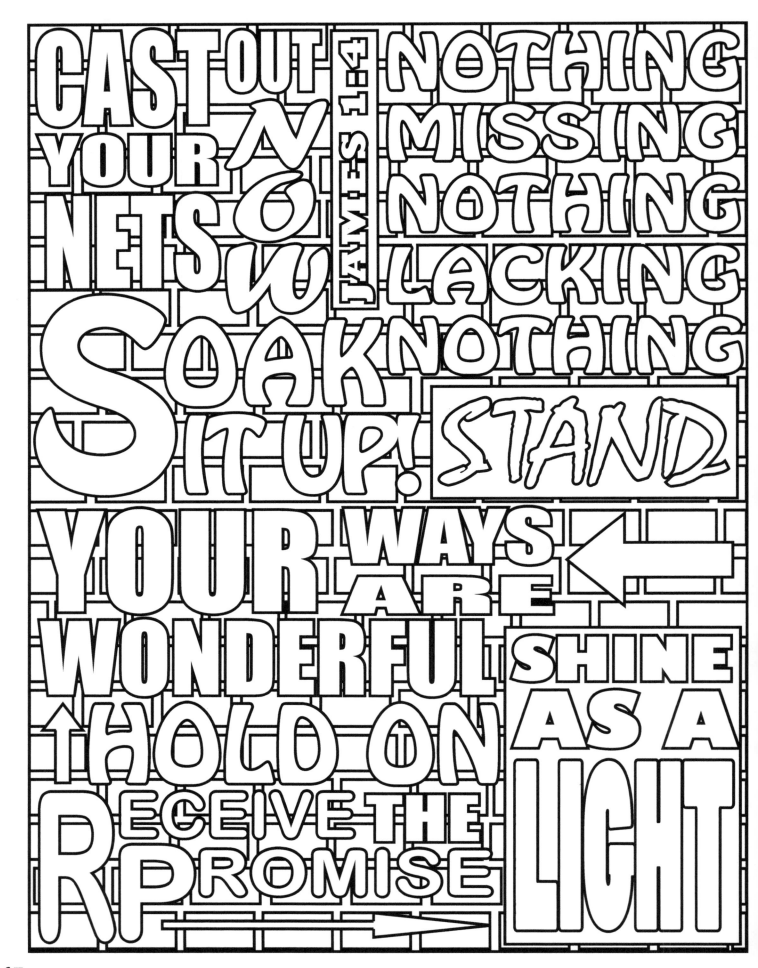

Worship GRaffiti

CAST OUT YOUR NETS

John 21:3-10

Who God says I am

(use your own graffiti to answer)

47

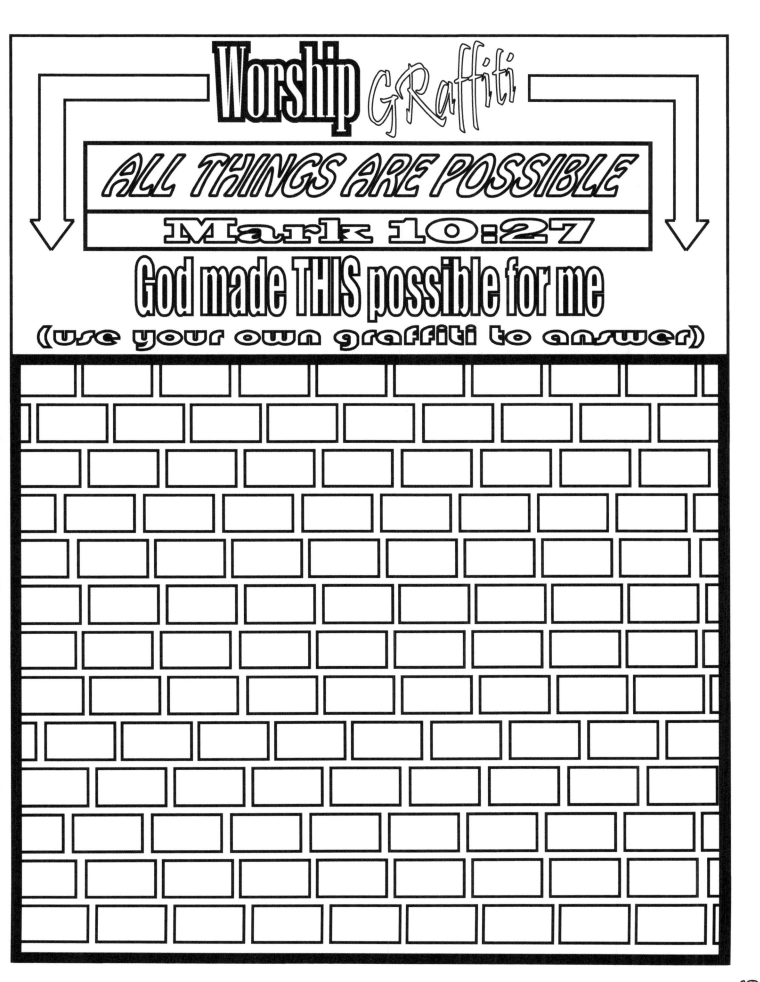

48

49

Worship GRaffiti

WAY MAKER

Matthew 19:26

How HE has made a way for ME...

(use your own graffiti to answer)

50

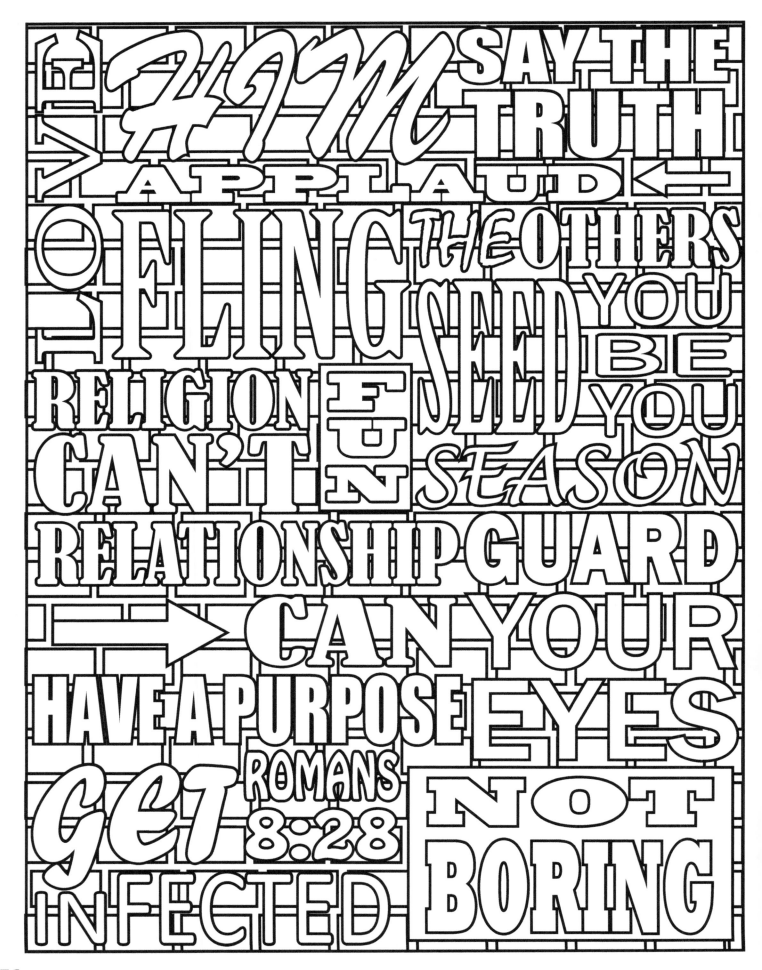

51

Worship GRaffiti

FLING THE SEED
Matthew 17:20

What mountains are your seeds MOVING?
(use your own graffiti to answer)

53

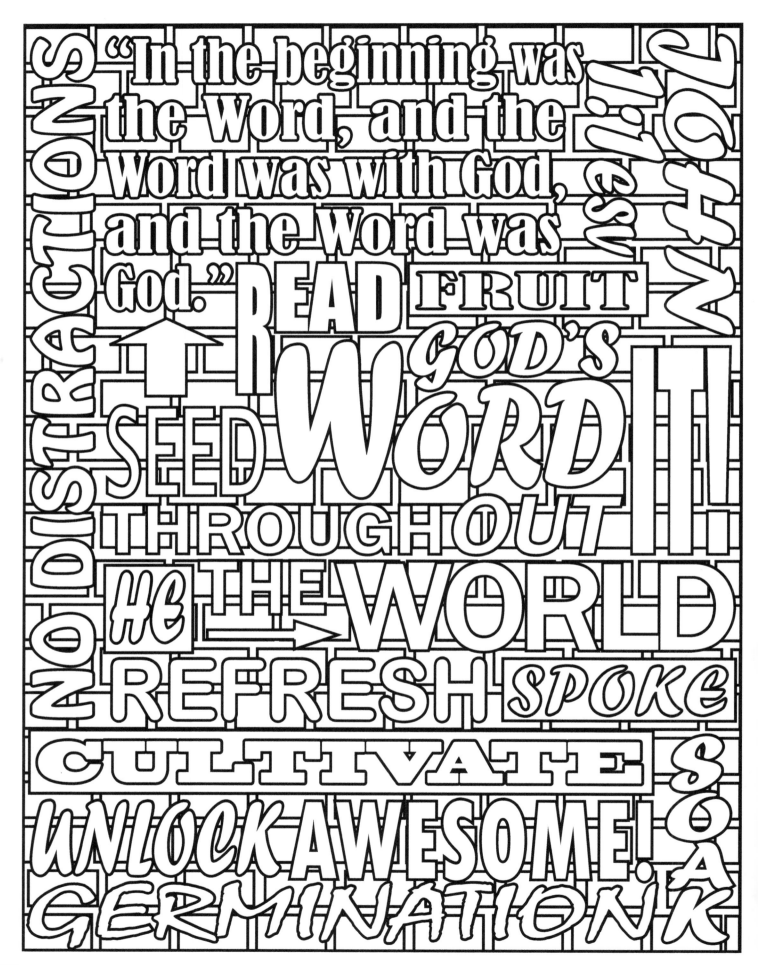

"In the beginning was the Word, and the Word was with God, and the Word was God." JOHN

READ FRUIT

SEED GOD'S WORD

THROUGHOUT

HE THE WORLD

REFRESH SPOKE

CULTIVATE

UNLOCK AWESOME!

GERMINATION

SOAK

NO DISTRACTIONS

Jesus lives!

55

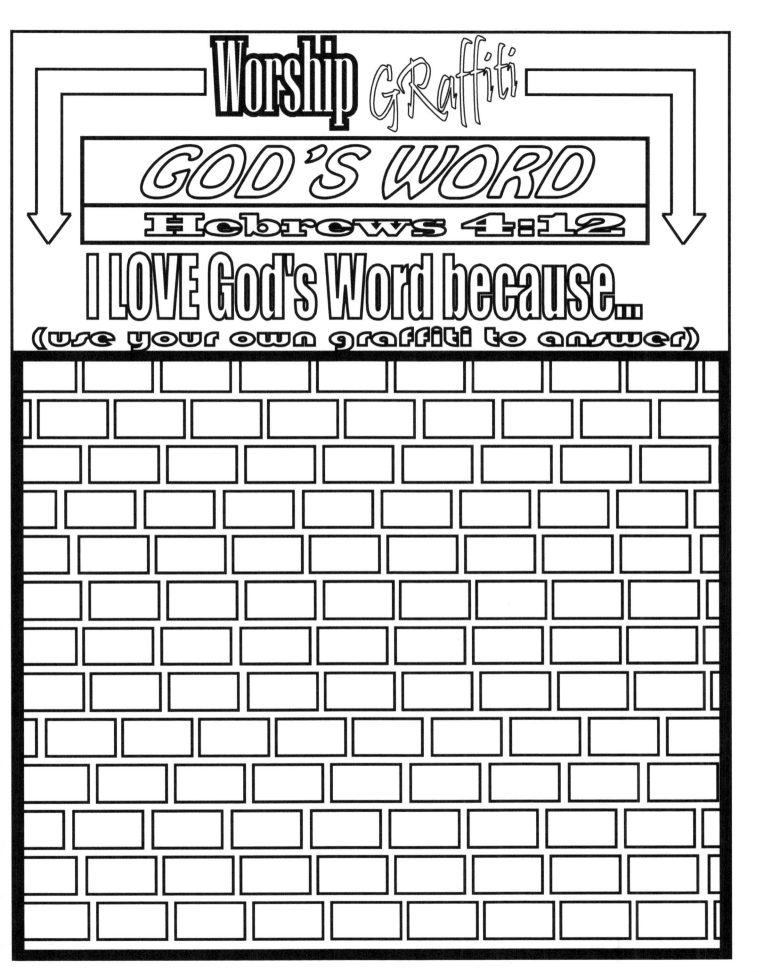

SERVE YAHWEH STICK TO IT!
GOD! BE AVAILABLE
IS ON THE CROSS
ABLE FULFILL
STAY! YOUR
AMAZED! PART
PUT ON THE IT'S IN
WHOLE THE
ARMOR BOOK
WHERE'S FOOD
THE VICTORY

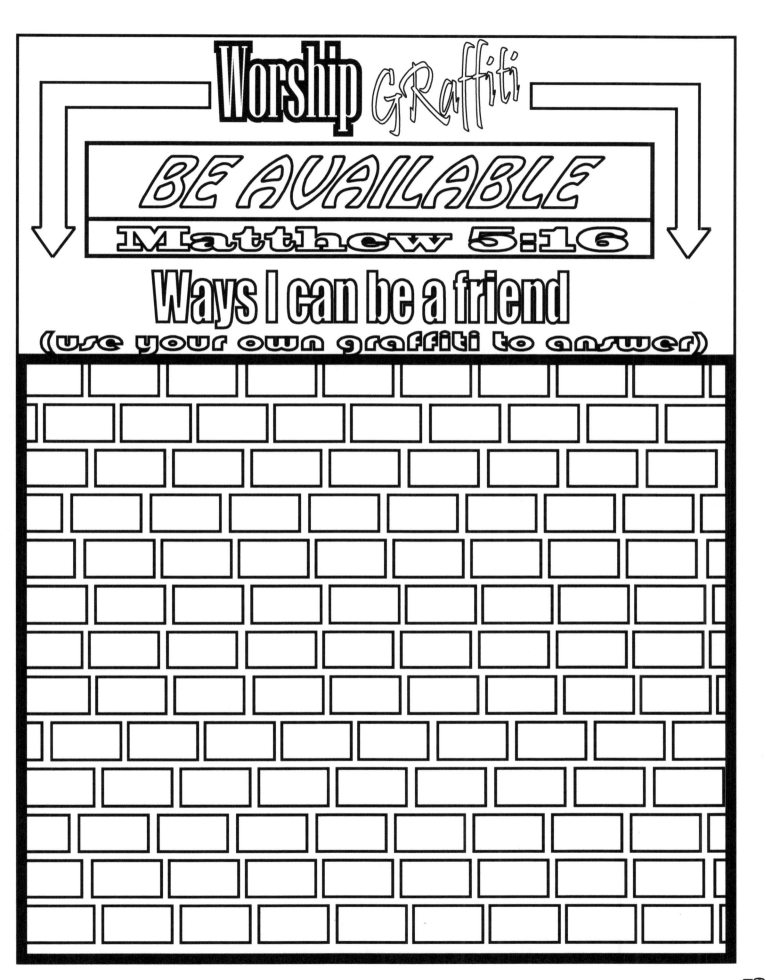

Worship GRaffiti

BE AVAILABLE
Matthew 5:16

Ways I can be a friend
(use your own graffiti to answer)

58

59

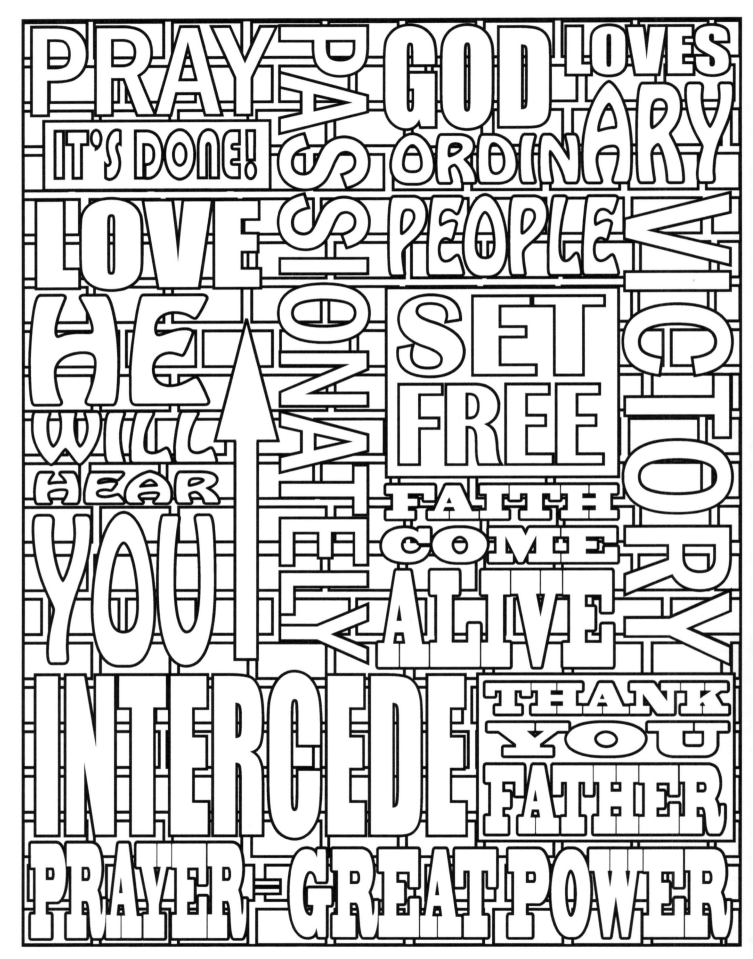

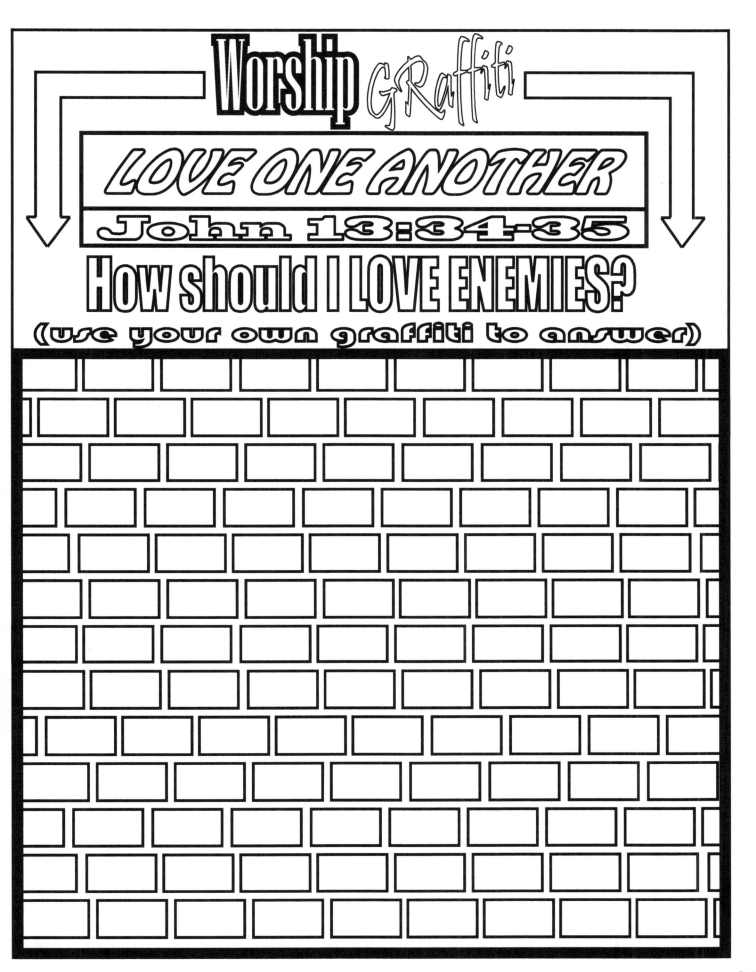

68

73

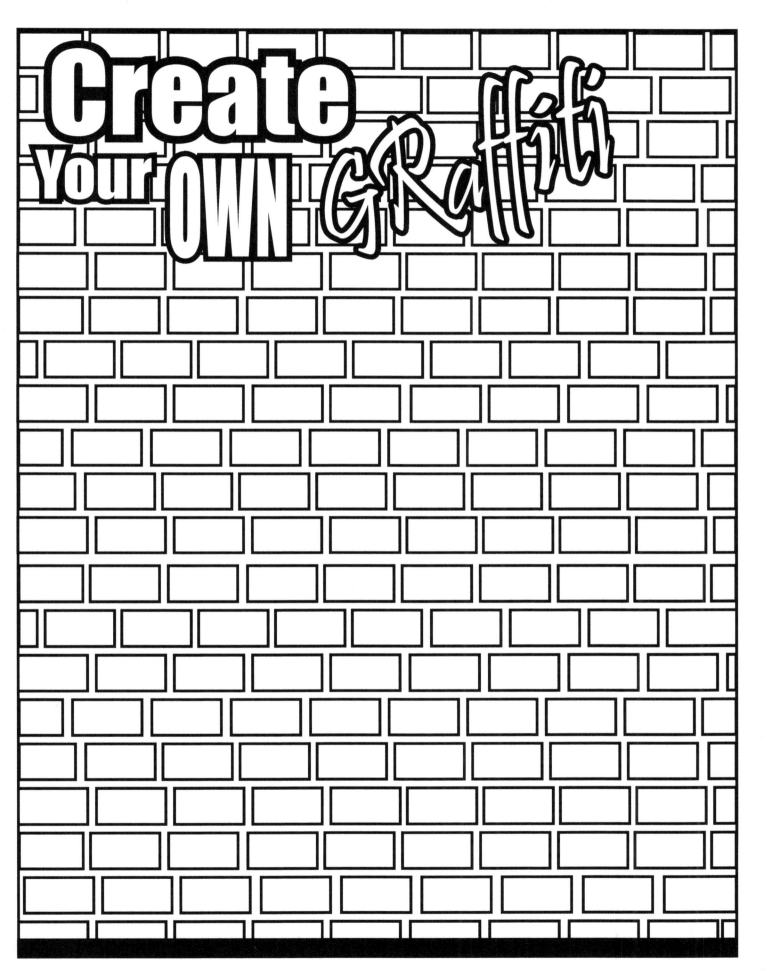

CPSIA information can be obtained
at www.ICGtesting.com
Printed in the USA
LVHW021508121220
673925LV00005B/314

9 781612 448862